IMAGES
of England

THE GUIDE
ASSOCIATION
IN CORNWALL

1st Tywardreath Guides, June 1926.

IMAGES
of England

THE GUIDE
ASSOCIATION
IN CORNWALL

Compiled by
Nicola Horne

To Pam,

*I hope you enjoy the memories
of many happy years of Guiding
in Cornwall.*

Best Wishes,

Nicola Horne

TEMPUS

Tempus Publishing Limited
The Mill, Brimscombe Port,
Stroud, Gloucestershire, GL5 2QG

ISBN 0 7524 2254 5

Typesetting and origination by
Tempus Publishing Limited
Printed in Great Britain by
Midway Colour Print, Wiltshire

Dedication

To everyone who has shared in the fun and friendship that Guiding in Cornwall has offered over the years.

Ann Trevenen Jenkin, the Cornish Grand Bard, with a group of Guides during the Millennium Festival Day at Stithians, June 2000.

Contents

Acknowledgements

I would like to express my sincere thanks to everyone who has made the publication of this book possible, including those who sent their treasured photographs to me, the photographers for providing permission for their photos to be included and the members of the County Executive for their support. I am sorry to be unable to name you all here. I would also like to say a special thank you to the following people who were invaluable in helping with the compilation of this book: Jane Bennett and Angela Thomas who not only greeted my initial idea for this book with enthusiasm, but continued to show their support throughout the last twelve months by giving up their time for meetings, helping with research and proof-reading. Margaret Jackson, the County Archivist, who has devoted many years to compiling the comprehensive albums of archive material that were so invaluable to me. I would like to thank Margaret for her commitment and expertise, as well as the help that her husband, John, has given in carrying the many heavy boxes of archive material! Lindsay Whittaker who accompanied me to numerous meetings, was a fresh pair of eyes when it was difficult to choose from the thousands of photographs and gave up many hours to discuss the captions over the phone! Sylvia Sanders, Nina Bunney and Grace Hocking for giving up their time to help with my research and for sharing some of their Guiding experiences with me. Finally, a big thank you must go to my family for encouraging and supporting my continued interest in Guiding. Thank you to Mum and Dad for their reliable taxi service over the years and to David for teaching me the time-saving skill of scanning photos. Thanks also to Gerard who not only put up with our house being taken over by thousands of photos but also spent many hours scanning the photos for me!

Thank you – One and All.

Introduction

I hope that the following introduction will serve to give a brief insight into the roots of The Guide Association for readers with little or no knowledge of the organization, as well as providing details on how Guiding began in Cornwall for those who have been involved over the years.

In 1907 Robert Baden-Powell held his first experimental camp for Boy Scouts on Brownsea Island, Dorset, where twenty boys joined together to try out his ideas for a programme of activities for boys. Following this successful camp, Baden-Powell went on to write *Scouting For Boys* describing the scheme he had devised, including the skills of camping, team work, leadership, pioneering and orienteering. Scouting was designed to prepare the boys with skills that may be useful as they grew older.

This book was read by girls as well as boys and soon they too wanted to be part of the growing Scout Movement. The Girl Guides were subsequently formed and a Scheme for Girl Guides was published. Together with his sister, Agnes, Baden-Powell wrote the first Guide Handbook, *How Girls Can Build Up The Empire*.

In 1910, the Girl Guide Association was formed and Agnes Baden-Powell took charge of this new Movement. The new Guides were awarded a certificate and Promise badge when they joined the Association, and spent their time practising first aid, signalling, drill and stretcher work. They also went camping, although often stayed in barns or village halls rather than sleeping in tents.

In 1914, the Brownies were formed enabling the younger sisters of the Girl Guides to take part in similar activities. At first this section of the Movement was known as Rosebuds however this name was not very popular and so was changed. By 1916, there were approximately 2,450 Brownies in the UK.

In 1912, Robert Baden-Powell married Olave Soames who became fully involved in her husband's work with the Scout Movement. In 1918, Olave was acclaimed Chief Guide and was presented with the highest award in Guiding, the Silver Fish.

In 1922, the Girl Guides were given a house in the New Forest as a gift of Mrs Archbold Sanderson. Foxlease, as it was called, soon became the first training centre for The Guide Association and is still a popular destination for Brownies, Guides and Guiders who visit for camps and training courses. Foxlease lies within the South West England Region and Cornish Guides and Guiders have enjoyed the friendships formed and ideas exchanged by fellow Guides and Guiders from around the UK and the world during many events and camps held there.

A new section of Guiding, the Rainbows, was introduced in 1987 to cater for girls younger than Brownies. Their Promise badges were similar to those of other sections of the Association and their uniform was a tabard in one of the colours of the rainbow.

The uniforms worn and badges gained by members of the Association have changed slightly over the years, but the Guide Association (as it is now known) has remained a popular youth organisation and continues to maintain the ideals of its founder, Robert Baden-Powell. Today, as the Association approaches its hundredth anniversary, it is the largest voluntary organisation for girls in the UK with 700,000 members.

Guiding in Cornwall was started early in 1910 by the Revd Walker and Miss Williams. Together they raised the interest of others and formed a committee which organised and subsidised the start of the 1st Cornwall Scout Troop. Florence Walker, Mr Walker's younger daughter, found six other keen girls who met in her house and worked for their Tenderfoot badges. Miss Walker, the elder daughter, acted as temporary Captain until a replacement was found.

The girls were enrolled on 10 June 1910 in Kimberley Park, Falmouth but were classed as Scouts and followed the Scout Handbook. They wore a uniform which consisted of khaki shorts and hats, navy-blue school skirts, black woollen stockings, black lace-up shoes and brown gauntlet gloves. They carried a haversack containing a first-aid kit, string, paper and pencil as well as a water bottle, billycan, whistle, knife and coil of rope.

Soon Miss Porter joined the group as their regular Captain with two Lieutenants, Miss Clatworthy and Miss Badger. This group of seven girls increased to a full Troop of three Patrols and their meetings were moved to a rented hall each Saturday afternoon. A Troop was later formed in Truro, led by Miss Earthy. When the Guide Movement was formed these Troops became Girl Guides and changed their uniform.

Cornwall Guide Association now boasts over 5,000 members who continue to enjoy activities and friendships in over 300 Rainbow, Brownie, Guide and Ranger Guide Units across the county.

I have looked at thousands of treasured photographs in order to compile this book and have been able to choose only 200 images to be published. Therefore this book can only scratch the surface of the memories of everyone who has been involved in Guiding in Cornwall since the founding days in 1910.

I hope that the images in this book are representative of the activities enjoyed by members of the Movement across the county and that they are able to prompt many happy memories for those who have been involved. I hope also that this book will be of interest to new and future members of Cornwall Guides who can discover more about the history of their Association.

Nicola Horne
July 2001

Foreword

What a wonderful record of achievement and happiness Guiding in Cornwall has been for so many people.

This book shows how valuable The Guide Movement is in the training of skills which we need in our daily lives and in its teaching of responsibility and duty to the young people who join the units in our county. It is splendid to see the names of the young as Brownies or Guides appearing again as Leaders and then again as Commissioners and finally as Members of the Trefoil Guild. It shows how very satisfying it is to be a member of The Guide Association and to make lifelong friends.

There is such fun enjoyed by those who are members of The Guide Association and being part of this Movement gives us the opportunity to work with Scouts and Guides from all over the world.

None of this would be possible if we did not have so many leaders who give so much of their time and energy to running the Association. We are all grateful to them as, I am sure, are all the parents.

May I wish the Guides in Cornwall continuing success and above all to have fun. Think back on the happy days spent in Guiding as a benchmark for what you can achieve in life!

Viscountess Falmouth
President of the Cornwall Guide Association
August 2001

Viscount and Viscountess Falmouth in High Cross, Truro, for the Service of Thanksgiving for the seven new Division Standards at Truro Cathedral in February 1992. The Standards were made following an anonymous donation to the County for the provision of the Standards.

Lady Baden-Powell with her daughter, Hon. Betty Clay, during their visit to the Isles of Scilly, *c.* 1961.

One

Guiding around the Country

Many towns and villages throughout Cornwall have been home to units of Rainbows, Brownies, Guides and Rangers over the years and so it seems appropriate to start this book with a selection of photographs which represent the many units from across the county. It is especially interesting to note how the uniforms have changed over the years since the time of this first photograph in 1919.

A training camp was held for Girl Guide Officers at Newquay County School during Easter 1919. Twenty-eight Guiders from around the county assembled to gain the training necessary to successfully run a Guide Company.

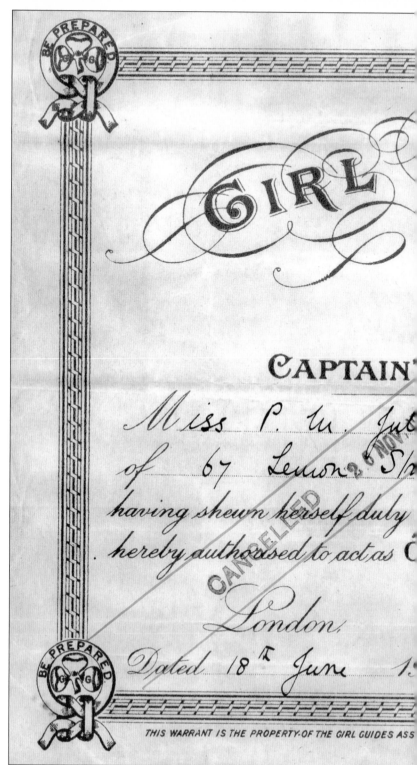

GIRL

CAPTAIN'

Miss P. M. Jul

of 67 Lemon St

having shewn herself duly

hereby authorised to act as C

London,

Dated 18th June 1

CANCELLED 26 NOV

THIS WARRANT IS THE PROPERTY OF THE GIRL GUIDES ASS

BE PREPARED

This Captain's Warrant, issued to Miss Julian in 1919, would have been one of the first in

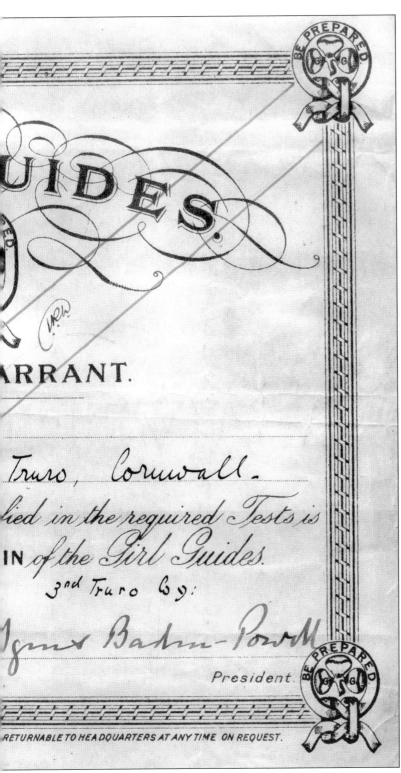

UIDES.

ARRANT.

Truro, Cornwall.

lied in the required Tests is
IN of the Girl Guides.

3rd Truro G:

Agnes Baden-Powell

President.

RETURNABLE TO HEADQUARTERS AT ANY TIME ON REQUEST.

the county.

1st Rosecraddoc Guide Company was formed in 1921 by Mrs Gibson of Rosecraddoc Manor. Later in 1927, the Rosecraddoc Brownies were formed. Back row, second from right: Mary Cock (2nd Lieutenant, Guides); fifth from right Ethel Whiting; sixth from right Sybil Hancock (Tawny Owl, Brownies); eighth from right May Stephens (1st Lieutenant, Guides) and Irene Tenouth; Millicent Hancock (Brown Owl, Brownies) and Mrs Gibson (Guide Captain).

1st Catchfrench Company of Girl Guides, c. 1920s.

Freda Hornabrook, Captain of the 1st Padstow Guide Company, probably on the beach in North Cornwall around the 1920s.

1st Boscastle Brownies, c. 1928.

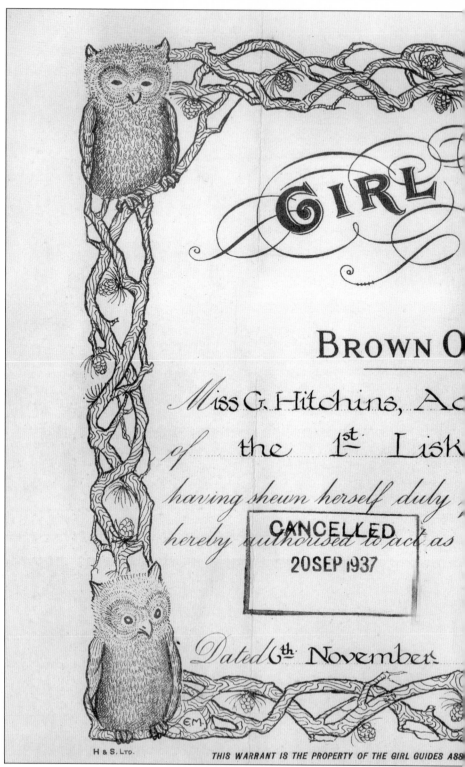

GIRL

BROWN O

Miss G. Hitchins, Ac

of   the   1st   Lisk

having shewn herself duly

hereby authorised to act as

CANCELLED
20 SEP 1937

Dated 6th November

THIS WARRANT IS THE PROPERTY OF THE GIRL GUIDES ASS

H & S. LTD.

Miss G. Hitchins was a long-serving member of the Guide Association in Liskeard.

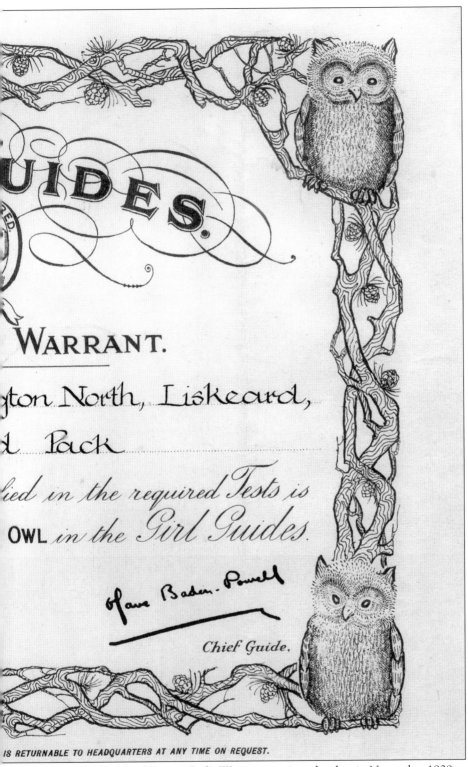

GUIDES.

WARRANT.

... gton North, Liskeard,

... Pack

...lied in the required Tests is

...OWL in the Girl Guides.

Olave Baden-Powell

Chief Guide.

IS RETURNABLE TO HEADQUARTERS AT ANY TIME ON REQUEST.

This ornately decorated Brown Owl's Warrant was issued to her in November 1929.

Miss W. Watkins, Bude and Miss N. Mitchell, Boscastle around the 1930s.

3rd Truro Guide Company at the Coronation Rally held in 1937.

Lady Baden-Powell with Lady Vivian MBE, March 1928. Lady Vivian was County Commissioner between 1931-1935 and served as the President of the Cornwall Guide Association between 1935-1948.

2nd Liskeard GFS (Girls Friendly Society) Guides in London for the Festival of Britain, 1951. Included are Mrs Rene Cornish and Miss Gladys Hitchens.

11th Falmouth Brownie Pack with Guiders Miss Joyce Taylor and Miss Diana Whitwam and Pack Leaders Valerie Choak and Angela Thomas, around April 1955.

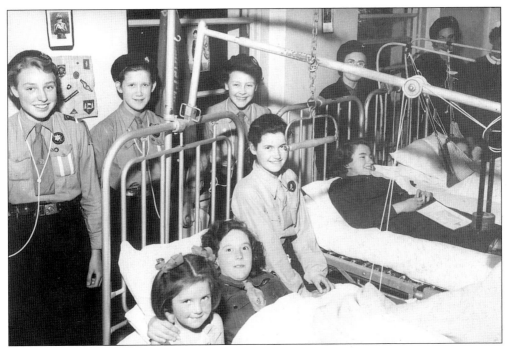

St Mary's Guides visiting the Guides in City Hospital, Truro around 1950s.

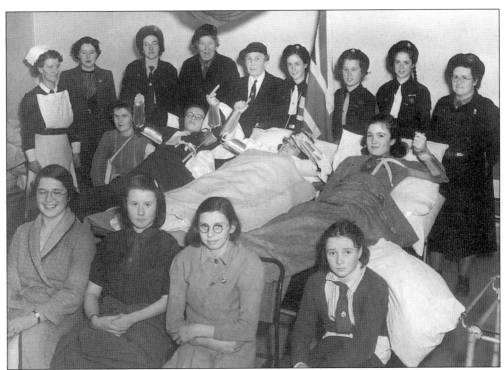

3rd Truro St George's Guides help with an enrolment for the Guide Company based at Truro City Hospital around early 1950s. Back row, from left to right: -?-, -?-, Mrs Doris Marriott, Miss Sally Butler, Mrs Read, Penny Marriott, May Jose, Jenny Marriott, Miss Grace Hocking.

The county's coastline has offered many advantages, including the formation of Sea Ranger units. These Sea Rangers, who were almost certainly from Penzance, can be seen sailing in their boat, the *Enterprise*.

SRS *Venus* Sea Rangers in Truro including Guider Miss Ena Coombe in the centre of the front row around 1965/66.

Penzance and Falmouth Sea Rangers at the first Culdrose Youth Sunday, 1966. Miss Valerie Mellor (Sea Ranger Guider, at front) and Shirley Masters (Guide Guider, near back).

SRS *Lyonesse* Sea Rangers, based in Penzance, receiving the Ranger International Certificate from Mrs Cynthia Johnson in September 1970. Miss Valerie Mellor and Mrs Annette Bowen (County Commissioner) are pictured on the right.

8th Truro, 12th Truro and Carnon Downs Guides visit Portscatho during a camp nearby. Included in this photograph are: Rosemary Barnes, -?-, Mary Cork, Phyllis Brown (St Paul's Guider), Nina Bunney, Mary Langdon, -?-, Joan Harding, ? Budden, Rosemary Anstis, Marguerite Lugg, Diana Way around early 1950s.

2nd Liskeard GFS Brownie Pack on Grammar School Field in 1967. Included, from left to right are: Carol Brassett (Pack Leader), Miss C. Moon (Tawny Owl), Hazel Spear (Guide) and Miss G. Hitchens (Brown Owl). (Photograph appears courtesy of Mr J. Rapson)

Guides from Truro District marching along Boscawen Street towards Truro Cathedral. Leading the parade are Mrs Mattie Phillips (District Commissioner), Mrs Honor Blair, Miss Grace Hocking and Miss Nina Bunney around late 1950s. Little has changed to the frontage of Woolworth's in the background and a coffee shop now occupies the Westminster Bank building.

Mrs Peggy Pascoe (Brown Owl) with the newly formed 1st Stithians Brownies in 1967.

Baldhu Brownies, formed in 1959, here with Mrs Judith Lobb and Mrs Annear around 1967.

St Newlyn East Brownies, Guides and Rangers presenting a seat for the community to celebrate the Diamond Jubilee of The Guide Association in 1970. Included in this photograph are Mrs Bowen (County Commissioner), Mrs Bellingham (Division Commissioner), A. Dunstan (District Commissioner), D. Appleton (Guide Guider) and Mrs Marks (Brownie Guider).

A church parade during a Guider's training weekend on the Isles of Scilly in September 1973.

1st St Austell Guides, April 1975.

3rd Truro (St George's Methodist) Guides and Brownies taking blackberry jelly and other produce to the Cathedral to raise money for Oxfam around 1970.

Liskeard Rangers, Guides and Brownies parading to St Martin's church for the Queen's Silver Jubilee Service in 1977.

Cawsand Brownies with Mrs Margaret Nichols during a pack holiday. The Brownies are wearing their Pack Holiday t-shirts and shorts with the trefoil in the middle around 1970s.

1st Wall Brownies during their first Promise evening in November 1977. Included from left to right are: Guiders B. Nicolaou, Mrs H. Caseley (District Commissioner), D. Whitehouse (Tawny Owl), B. Mitchell (Snowy Owl) and Kay Cook (Brown Owl). Along with Brownies, from left to right: Ann-Marie Carswell, Tracey Williams, Tanya Atkins, Kerenza Busfield, Victoria Goom, Kirsten Mitchell, Naomi Connon, Sarah Broughton, Paula Cook, Esther Connon, Marie Riches and Kelly Hampton.

5th St Austell Rangers (Extensions) during a trip to Bodrugan Farm in May 1978. Back row, from left to right: Mary ?, Nina Mitchell, Pat ?, Ann ?, Front row, from left to right: Susan ?, Jill ?, Valerie ?, Sharon ?.

A National Song Contest, organized with the help of the BBC, was held in London in 1972. Members of the 11th Truro (St Johns) Guides, seen here, represented the South West England Region during the final of the Guide Choir Section, where they came second. (Photograph appears courtesy of Mr J. Warburton)

A Brownie, pictured with Carole Gardner, enjoying the challenge of building the biggest tower during the Restormel Round-up day in July 1981.

3rd Penryn (St Gluvias Church) Brownies, c. 1973. Included are Mrs Dulcie Blackmore (Brown Owl) and Miss Susan Prout (Tawny Owl).

Saltash Brownies at Saltash Guide Headquarters, *c.* 1980. With the Brownies are, from left to right: Barbara Gilbert, Betty Page, Pauline Samuel, -?-, Ann Hine, Joan Lamerton and Angela Thomas.

10th Falmouth Guides gather together for a presentation of Queens Guide Awards to, from left to right: Barbara Lewis, Allison Moyle, Joanne Bonney, Tracey Williams and Danila Green. The Guiders pictured are Pauline Moyle and Jane Bennett with Young Leader Sarah Bennett around 1984.

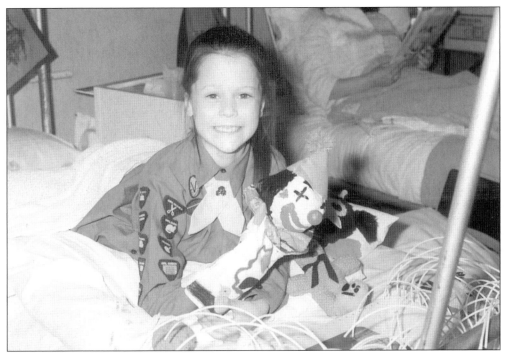

Victoria Geach from Launceston continues her Brownie activities during her stay in Mount Gould Hospital around the 1970s.

1st Par Guides in concert at Gott Hall, Par in 1982.

St Cleer and Menheniot Guides during their activity sleepover in 1997.

Grace Saydon, Rebecca Symons, Rebecca Dobson and Kimberley Matthews from 3rd Falmouth (Bosvale) Rainbows with the Rainbow Arch during a Promise-making ceremony.

Members of the newly formed Truro Gloweth Action Plus unit receiving the flag donated to them by The Bush Telegraph Co. UK Ltd, April 1999. Back row, from left to right: Laura Mitchell, Kate Nightingale, Lucy Falkner, Nicola Horne (Guider), Sally Horne (Director, The Bush Telegraph Co UK Ltd). Front Row, from left to right: Jessica Anderson, Hayley Augarde, Lisa Goodman.

Trefoil Guild members enjoying the Millennium Festival Day at Stithians Showground in June 2000.

1st Budock Brownies presenting books donated to the Book Aid appeal to Rotarians Mr Rod Allday and Mr Ian Newman, December 1999. Back row, from left to right: Lucy King, Katie Smith, Samantha Reid, Mr Rod Allday, Ian Newman, Zoe Symons, Naomi Morant, Mrs Pauline Allday (Brownie Guider), Jessica Lait. Front row, from left to right: Stephanie Lait, Charlotte Wells, Sally Morrison, Lauren Roberts, Amy Roberts, Coral Andrewartha, Emily Jorey and Rebecca Higham.

Two Brownies from 8th Falmouth enjoying their sponsored Readathon in Kimberley Park, Falmouth in July 2000.

Two
Awards and
Presentations

Guides in Cornwall have been successful in completing the wide range of challenging badges and awards that are included in the Guide Programme. Proficiency badges were introduced in the early days of Guiding and subsequently Guides have enjoyed gaining the knowledge necessary for their First Class, Queen's Guide and Baden-Powell Awards. There have also been a number of presentations recognising bravery and service by members of Guiding in Cornwall, a small selection of which are also included in this chapter.

The Laurel Award is given in recognition of outstanding service to Guiding. The award is a silver medallion surrounded by a green enamelled laurel wreath. The sapphire-blue ribbon has two green stripes bordering a central white stripe. Miss Angela Thomas (County Commissioner) is receiving the Laurel Award from Lady Falmouth at a presentation in 1992. Also, from left to right: Mrs Myra Bellingham, Mrs Jill Kendall, Mrs Helen Caseley and Mrs Pauline Samuel.

The Queen's Guide Award was introduced in 1946. Patricia Williams is receiving her Queen's Guide Award from Mrs Phyllis Read (Assistant County Commissioner) at Penzance in 1963.

Janet Appleton receiving her Queen's Guide Award from Lady St Aubyn in Truro. Also, from left to right: Mrs Cynthia Johnson, -?-, Susan Mischler (Standard Bearer), Mrs Mattie Phillips, Catherine Hardy around the late 1950s early 1960s.

Pam Page and Patricia Dobson of Liskeard Guides receive their Queen's Guide Awards in 1961. Also in the back row, from left to right: Mrs B. Page, Mrs E. Dobson and Mrs A. Bowen (County Commissioner).

Patricia Cardell and Ruth Goldsworthy with Mrs A. Bowen (County Commissioner) after receiving the first two Queen's Guide Awards gained by 1st Leedstown Guide Company, February 1968. (Photograph appears courtesy of *Western Morning News*)

Mandy Ruse, from 8th Truro Guides, receiving her Queen's Guide Award from Mrs Pat Hammett (Division Commissioner, Carrick North). Also, from left to right: Pat Joll, Gill Harris and Nina Bunney around 1976.

Nine Guides from the 2nd Liskeard GFS Guides following the presentation of the Queen's Guide Awards around the 1970s. From left to right: Susan Atkins, Katherine Matthews, Felicity Pilditch, Alison Symons, Nicola Martin, Nicola Jewson, Teresa Wilton, Lorraine Wilton and Denise Lamer. (Photograph appears courtesy of Mr J. Rapson)

Katy Grint receives her Queen's Guide Award from Miss Mary Timpson (Division Commissioner, Carrick South) watched by Miss Doreen Burtt (Guide Guider, 1st Mawnan Guides).

Guides learnt skills such as knot-tying, first-aid, cooking out-of-doors and were tested at their weekly meetings. They were able to progress from being a Tenderfoot, to gaining their Second Class and First Class badges. In this photo Judith Soloman and Ann Tinney of 8th Truro (St Mary's Guides) receive their first-class badges from Mrs Mattie Phillips (Truro District Commissioner) watched by Miss Nina Bunney, March 1964. (Photograph appears courtesy of the *Western Morning News*)

Carol Brassett receives her First-Class and All-Round cords from Mrs Doris Travers, (District Commissioner, Liskeard) 1965. (Photograph appears couresy of Mr J. Rapson)

The syllabus for the Queen's Guide Award was amended in 1983 when it became an award for members of the Senior Section. The Baden-Powell Trefoil was introduced for the Guide Section. Hannah Critchley of 1st Liskeard Guides is receiving her Baden-Powell Award from Mayor Mrs Joan Moffat, watched by Kath Hawes (District Commissioner, Liskeard) and Margaret Jackson (Division Commissioner) in February 1987. (Photograph appears couresy of Mr J. Rapson)

Claire Day receiving her Baden-Powell Award from Joyce Crooks (County International Advisor) watched by Margaret Jackson (Caradon Division Commissioner) and the 2nd Liskeard Guides, November 1988. (Photograph appears couresy of Mr M. Mort)

Her Royal Highness Princess Margaret, President of the Guide Association, holds an annual reception for those girls who have received the new Queen's Guide Award. Nicola Horne, Kate Simpson and Anita Parsons are at Guide Association Headquarters in London with their Queen's Guide Awards following the reception and presentation at Kensington Palace in April 1995.

Sarah Barrett receives her Queen's Guide Award from Jane Bennett (County Commissioner) in 1998. (Photograph appears couresy of Mr R. Dovey)

Tamzin Puttock receives her Queen's Guide Award from Jane Bennett (County Commissioner) in 1998. (Photograph appears couresy of Neale & Neale)

The Star of Merit is awarded to uniformed members of the association who have displayed great courage or fortitude, or have shown great initiative or responsibility at an incident. This photograph shows the Presentation of the Star of Merit for outstanding bravery in illness to Carly Durham of Launceston Guides by Angela Thomas (County Commissioner) in January 1994.

The presentation of the Star of Merit for outstanding bravery in illness to Hannah Coombe of St Austell Brownies by Angela Thomas (County Commissioner). Also, from left to right: Mrs Coombe (Hannah's mother) and Paula Ellis (Brownie Guider) around June 1994. (Photograph appears couresy of Mr Harry Barrett)

Presentation of the Star of Merit for outstanding bravery in illness to Marianne Kitchener of Camborne Brownies by Angela Thomas (County Commissioner).

Five members of the Cornwall Trefoil Guild were among those who received the 1994 Royal Maundy Money from Her Majesty The Queen at Truro Cathedral. They were Miss Nina Bunney, Doreen Burtt (pictured centre), Miss Grace Hocking, Miss Betty Martin and County Vice-President Mrs Florence Christie (far right). The Queen presents the Royal Maundy money each Easter. Traditionally, the number of people chosen to receive the Maundy money depends on the age of the monarch, hence in 1994, sixty-eight men and sixty-eight women were presented with Maundy purses. The white purse contains silver Maundy coins adding up to the age of the sovereign. The red purse contains £5.50 for clothing, provisions and for the 'redemption of the royal gown.'

The Bolitho Shield was first presented in 1921 to the 1st Devoran Guide Company, seen here with Captain Miss M.D. Tyack. The shield was donated by Mrs Agnes Bolitho of Trengwainton, Penzance and has been competed for by Guides within the county since that date, excluding a gap for war-time years.

3rd Saltash Guides and Mrs Jill Kendall (County Commissioner) with the Bolitho Shield in 1988.

The Halford Trophy, here being held by the 1st Liskeard Brownies alongside Mrs Angela Thomas and Mrs Valerie Paytress, was first presented in the late 1970s. Mrs Sheen, a Brownie Guider and the County Registrations Secretary, introduced the trophy to enable Brownies around the county to compete against each other in a similar way to the Bolitho Shield for Guides and Margot Rogers Cup for Rangers. The trophy was carved by Mr Tony Dunstan and a base added by Mrs Sheen's husband.

The Margot Rogers Cup was donated to the Cornwall Guide Association by Mrs Margot Rogers (County Commissioner 1936-1949, County President 1949-1959) in 1950. The cup was originally an Oxford Challenge Rowing Cup awarded to a member of Mrs Rogers' family. It is now competed for by Rangers around the county every three years. It is being held here by Falmouth Rangers, the winners in 1981. Also, included are: Mrs Barbara Gilbert, Mrs Margaret Dan, Mrs Joy Nodder, Mrs Doreen Burtt and Miss Pauline Samuel (County Commissioner).

Paula Hutchings, Carol Craddick and Christine Symons receiving the GFS Brownie All England Shield from the Mayor of Liskeard Mr Gilbert around the early 1950s. In the background is Mrs Gilbert, Mayoress.

Liskeard GFS Guides with the All England GFS Guide Shield that they won in 1948. Back row, from left to right: Margaret Brooks, Margaret Harris, Sylvia Healy, Pat Richardson and Margaret Arthur. Middle row, from left to right: Rita Hill (with colours), Yvonne Hosken, Celia Woodford, Julie Pearce, Rosemary Edmonds, Eileen Bennett, Annette Lock, -?-, Rhona Crews, Shirley Woodford (holding Union Jack). Front row, from left to right: Marie Davey, Margaret Dyer, Miss G. Hitchens (Lieutenant), Miss Harwood (District Commissioner), Mrs Cornish (Captain), Pauline Moon, Sheila Ough.

Three
Celebrations and Special Occasions

There have been many special occasions and anniversaries celebrated by Cornish Guides, a selection of which are included here. These range from county occasions, such as the dedication of the County and Division Standards, to the anniversaries celebrated in individual units. This chapter illustrates the diversity of occasions that the Cornish Guide Association have played host to over the years.

A procession through Truro of Girl Guides from around the county, prior to the dedication of the new County Standard in Truro Cathedral, by the Bishop of Truro in June 1956. From left to right: Jill Rookley and Heather Marriott (flag escorts) and on the far right: Ann Dunstan (Parade Marshall). (Photograph appears courtesy of the *Western Morning News*)

The seven Division Standards of Cornwall (North Cornwall, Restormel, Carrick North, Penwith, Kerrier, Carrick South, Caradon Cotehele and Caradon Tamar) together outside Truro Cathedral after a service of thanksgiving in February 1992.

On previous page: The County Standard was a gift of the County President, Vice-Presidents and Friends. It is present at County gatherings, denoting the presence of the County Commissioner. At the hoist of the Standard is the World Flag, the two stars symbolize our Promise and Law. The vein, or compass needle, is set to give us our true course in Guiding. The base of the stalk is a copy of the heraldic *Feu* and represents the flame of the love of mankind. The golden trefoil represents the sun shining in the blue sky, which is over all the Guides and Girl Scouts of the world. Next comes the Arms of the county of Cornwall. The black shield on a white field, with the fifteen golden bezants. The shield is surmounted by a coronet, showing that Cornwall is a Royal Duchy. The story of the bezants is generally believed to date back to the thirteenth century. Richard, brother of Henry III and Earl of Cornwall, fighting in the Crusades, was taken prisoner and – like his uncle, Richard Coeur de Lion before him – held to ransom. The ransom had to be paid in bezants – the gold coin of Byzantium – and the story goes that his faithful vassals in Cornwall collected and paid the whole ransom in the necessary coinage. 'One and all' contributed hence the County Motto, which appears on the Standard. The Guide Motto reminds us of our Founder, Lord Baden-Powell. The Celtic cross is typical of Cornwall, the land of saints. The Choughs, so well known by name and now so rarely seen, are shown on the fly, being the birds which are always linked in fact and fiction with Cornwall. Finally, the Sword of Excalibur shows the link between King Arthur and his Knights, who symbolize the ideals of chivalry summed up in our Guide Laws.

The South West England Region Standard, held here by Jill Kendall and Mia Girling. The Standard includes images of the World Trefoil Badge, The Cross of St George for England, The Cross of Christianity, The Golden Dragon of Wessex, a sailing ship for our seafaring tradition, The Guide Motto – 'Be Prepared', The English Rose and the Acorn of the English Oak, The Lion of the Norman Channel Islands and The Cornish Bezants.

Mary Eddy is presented with the Commissioner's Warrant as she begins her term as the first District Commissioner for Lands End. Also, from left to right: Ruth Corin, Helen Caseley, Barbara Nicolaou and Angela Thomas (County Commissioner), August 1996.

A group of Rangers with Mrs Mia Girling (Ranger Guider), Mrs Thelma Crocker (District Commissioner, Fowey and Lostwithel) and Mrs Jill Kendal (County Commissioner) at Fowey Harbour following their investiture around 1990.

During the Second World War, the Girl Guides raised money to help with the war effort. Guides across the country raised £50,000 which bought two air ambulances, twenty naval ambulances and a motor lifeboat. The lifeboat, then known as ON826, was called to help in the evacuation of troops from Dunkirk. It made two trips to France, and in 1947 was named *The Guide of Dunkirk* in recognition of her help in that evacuation. *The Guide of Dunkirk* was welcomed to Cornwall in 1947 as a serving lifeboat at Cadgwith. From left to right: Lady Vivian (County President) and Mrs Margot Rogers (County Commissioner).

In 1963 the boat was taken out of commission from the lifeboat service.

Girl Guides and Girl Scouts around the world celebrate Thinking Day on 22 February each year to coincide with the birthdays of Lord and Lady Baden-Powell. On this day Guides, Brownies and Rainbows celebrate the international aspect of Guiding and think of their fellow Girl Guides and Girl Scouts around the world.

The Golden Jubilee Thinking Day Party took place at St John's Hall, Penzance in 1960. Some of the 500 Guides and Brownies who joined together for the party from the West and South Divisions incorporating the areas around St Ives, Hayle, Penzance, Helston and the Lizard are gathered here. The Guides and Brownies are dressed in costumes of the member countries of the World Association of Girl Guides and Girl Scouts (WAGGGS). Also from left to right: the Mayor of Penzance, Councillor St Peake – cutting the birthday cake with the Mayoress – Mrs Williams, Mrs J. Read, Mrs Wooldridge, Miss Crankshaw and Miss Vickery.

In 1978, at the annual Thinking Day Serice at Westminster Abbey, London Mrs Sue Bellingham carried the standard in the colour party for the Chief Comissioner, Mrs Owen Walker.

Guides and Brownies from the Central Division took part in a Thinking Day ceremony held in the annexe of Truro City Hall in 1957. This ceremony coincided with the centenary of the birth of Lord Baden-Powell. Here the Guides light the candles as they remember the Girl Guides and Girl Scouts from countries around the world.

Truro District Guides and Brownies join together to take part in their Thinking Day ceremony held in St Mary's Methodist Hall in 1962. (Photograph appears courtesy of the *Western Morning News*)

Kerrier Division celebrated the centenary of Lady Baden-Powell's birth in 1989 with a special

service at Gwennap Pit.

In memory of Lady Baden-Powell, the members of the Trefoil Guild planted a rose-bed in the Waterfall Gardens, Truro. At the dedication of the rose-bed, from left to right: Lady Falmouth (President, Cornwall Guide Association), Mrs Chadwick (former County Trefoil Guild Chairman), Mrs Maundrell (County Trefoil Guild Chairman), Dr Ansari (Deputy Mayor's husband), Mrs Ansari (Deputy Mayor, Truro) Revd K. Rogers, -?-, Mrs C. Johnson and Mrs M. Bellingham (County Commissioner).

The members of the Trefoil Guild following the dedication of the rose-bed. Sadly, the rose-bed no longer exists in the Waterfall Gardens however the commemorative plaque can still be found within Victoria Gardens.

The first World Conference to be held in Britain since 1930, was held in Oxford in 1950. It was decided that each different country's party should be given a Scroll of Friendship which was passed to members of the Association on its journey to Oxford, accompanied by two log books. From left to right: Mrs Garrard, Mrs Travers and Leslie Smith with the scroll in Cornwall, 7 May 1950.

One of the two log books recorded the journey that the scroll made to the Conference, whilst the other contained the names of all those Brownies, Guides and Rangers who helped to carry the scroll to Oxford. The scrolls were carried in cardboard cylinders and protected by a 'Guide-blue' linen bag. Included, from left to right: Mrs B. Page, Diana Lock, Mary O'Brien, Jenny Ough, Margaret May and Bridget Doney.

Diana Chaplin hands the scroll to Miss Bettridge (Captain of Bodmin Guides) after carrying it from Lostwithiel.

1st Liskeard Guides handing the scroll to 2nd Liskeard GFS Guides.

Jane Curry and Penzance Guides pass on the Friendship Scroll, overlooking the sea.

In 1953, the Queen's Coronation was celebrated by Guides and Brownies across Cornwall. Brownies of the Central Divisions held a rally at County School in Truro. On the left: Miss Portsmore from Camborne, the County Brownie Trainer.

The Coronation rally, also took place in the main hall of County School. Included: Mrs Appleton, Miss Bell, Miss Graves, Miss Butler and Miss Coombe. (Photographs appear courtesy of the *Western Morning News*)

Angela Thomas presenting two benches to celebrate the Queen's Coronation on behalf of 11th Falmouth Guides outside Earle's Retreat, Falmouth in 1953.

Guides and Brownies from all over Cornwall joined together at RNAS Culdrose on 30 May 1970 to celebrate the Diamond Jubilee of the Guide Association. Along with a commemorative service, the Guides also enjoyed dressing in costumes that depicted the coming of Christianity to Cornwall.

There were a number of celebrations around the country to mark the seventy-fifth anniversary of Guiding in 1985. One of these celebrations included the lighting of a candle on the forecourt of Buckingham Palace; which was distributed to County Commissioners throughout the country. Here, Pauline Samuel (County Commissioner) and Jean Eburne (South West England Chief Commissioner) are lighting a candle on the platform of Truro railway station.

On 25 June 1985, Guides, Brownies and former members of the association joined together to plant a beech tree at Addington, Liskeard to commemorate the seventy-fifth anniversary. Miss G. Hitchens, a member of the Guide Movement in Liskeard for many years, is in the centre. (Photograph appears courtesy of Mr M. Mort)

A time capsule was compiled as a momento of the seventy-fifth year of Guiding and was received by Margaret Flinders and Helen Caseley at RNAS Culdrose in 1985.

The Caradon Division camp was held at Bindown where the Guides stood together in the shape of a trefoil to mark the seventy-fifth anniversary.

Nina Bunney with the 8th Truro Guides as they celebrate their twenty-first birthday in 1957. One of the many unit anniversaries that have been celebrated within the county.

12th Truro (St Pauls) Guides gathered together on 2 May 1957 to celebrate their Silver Jubilee.

Alison Armstrong, Denise Child, Sarah Wilcox and Janet Nash celebrate the forty-fifth anniversary of 1st Liskeard Brownies in 1974.

1st Mawnan Smith Brownies celebrate their twenty-first anniversary in 1990. Back row, from left to right: Margaret Gardner, Chris Grint, Hazel Gundrey, Doreen Burtt, Mary Owen, Catherine Allday, Pauline Allday. Third row, from left to right: Anna Mills,-?-,-?-, Helen Caunter. Second row, from left to right: Rosemary Dugdave, Alison Benney, Isobel Popple, Kimberley Grace, Jenna Rowe, Chloe Carrick,-?-, Penny Robson, Morwenna Hurst, Kirsty Nancholas. Front row, from left to right: Virginia Walker, Fleur and Samantha Bunyan, Katie Smith, Miranda Williams, Helen Benney, Gillian Matthews, Simone Devlin.

Threemilestone Brownies celebrate their twenty-fifth anniversary in June 2000. Back row, from left to right: Miss Lindsay Whittaker (Brown Owl), Kerry Marriott, Rachel James, Sarah Trebilcock, Victoria Thomas, Emma Peters, Amy Dunstan, Dawn Sutton, Emily Hinkley, Ciara Reddington, Alice Trevail, Miss Valerie Nankivell (Barn Owl). Front row, from left to right: Jessie Vallance, Katie Bowen, April Pinfield, Charlotte Makin, Becky Makin, Joanna Bunt, Bethany Lane, Milly Trevail, Cara Searle.

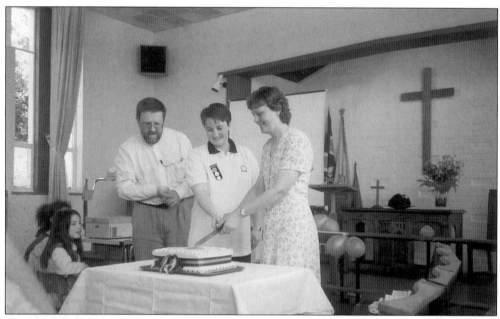

Cutting the cake at a thanksgiving service held at Threemilestone church during the weekend of anniversary celebrations at Threemilestone is Miss Nicola Horne (Snowy Owl) and Mrs Gill Harris (first Brown Owl at Threemilestone in 1975), watched by Brownie Charlotte Makin and Revd David Rhymer in June 2000.

Carrick South Brownies are gathered together for a Brownie Birthday Bonanza celebrating seventy years of Brownies in May 1989.

Rainbows from Restormel Division celebrated the tenth anniversary of Rainbows in May 1997.

Opening of the new Bodmin District Guide Hall by Mrs Myra Bellingham (County Commissioner) on Thinking Day 1974. Also included: Mrs Sparks, Mrs Joyce Skea, Margaret Taft (District Commissioner), Mr Pettybridge, Mrs Barbara Illsley, Ken Moore, ? Sparrow, Mrs Audrey Moore, Mrs Betty Bolton and Mrs Browning (Division Commissioner).

Opening of the Liskeard District Guide Headquarters at Luxstowe in June 1976. From left to right: George Walters (Lions Club President), Mr Robert Hicks MP, Margaret Jackson (Liskeard District Commissioner) and Miss Gladys Hitchens (Brown Owl, Liskeard Brownies).

The Brownie Guard of Honour at the wedding of Mrs Iris Harwood (District Commissioner for Liskeard 1944-48) around the late 1930s.

Mrs Dorothy Croxford is joined by Guiders on her wedding day in June 1923.

Mrs Bernice Gregg, Captain of 11th Falmouth Guides, here on her wedding day in 1956 with some of the Guides forming a Guard of Honour.

Liskeard Brownies and Guides gather together to form a Guard of Honour at the wedding of their Guide Captain Margaret Dyer to John Jackson on 3 September 1960.

1st Baldhu Brownies form a Guard of Honour at the wedding of their Tawny Owl, Judy Lobb, in 1963. Back row, from left to right: Janet Chegwidden, Lyn Chegwidden, Judith Wills, Lynette Christophers, Caroline Carlyon. Front row, from left to right: Patricia Wills, Margaret Wills, Jennifer Woolcock, Jennifer Rabey, Barbara Phillips, Susan Budge, Diana Wills, Shirley Rabey, ? Harris.

The Guides of the Messenger Service at the Royal Cornwall Show after forming a Guard of Honour for Her Majesty The Queen in June 2000.

Regular members of the Messenger Service Team at the Royal Cornwall Show taken in June 1998. From left to right: Rosemary Howells, Coralie Goodfellow, Elizabeth Legg and Jenny Treadwell.

Pam Jasper has catered for the Messenger Service at the Royal Cornwall Show for over twenty-five years and is seen here in June 1998.

In 1990 a new uniform, designed by Jeff Banks to be more practical and versatile, was launched. Members of Saltash District modelled the new uniform when it first became available.

The Guide Association is always keen to gain new members of all ages. Jessica Richardson from 3rd Falmouth (Bosvale) Rainbows took part in 'Guiding in Cornwall Week' in November 1999, keen to promote Guiding to any potential new adult members.

Four
Camps, Pack Holidays and Jamborees

Camping is one of the activities that has been enjoyed by Guides all over the world and the Cornish Guides are no exception. Units of Brownies and Guides from around the county have enjoyed many nights spent away from home under canvas or in local village halls and some have had the opportunity to represent their county during international camps. Although the tents used by the girls seem to have changed little over the years, the following photographs indicate that the means of transport used to get to camp and the facilities available to the Guides may have seen improvements.

The 1st Tywardreath, 1st Lostwithiel and 2nd Fowey Guides make their way home from camp on the back of this lorry in August 1924.

Penzance Guides get ready to leave for camp on the back of this horse and cart with their Guider Jane Curry in the 1950s.

This horse drawn carriage, the Truro-Devoran-Redruth Express, looks full to the brim of Guides on their way either to camp or a day out around 1920s.

2nd Liskeard GFS Guides off to camp in a lorry in 1960.

Valerie Mellor makes good use of this trolley to pull some camp equipment along the platform of Penzance Railway Station around the 1980s.

August 1921, the first Guiders camp was held by Guiders from Bude and Launceston at Tiscott Farm, Poughill near Bude.

The Patrol Leaders from 1st Catchfrench Guide Company on camp in August 1921.

In 1924, Launceston Guiders had their annual camp in Werrington Park. The Guiders camped overnight and the Brownies visited during the day. Miss Watkins (Captain at Poughill) was in charge at the camp, assisted by Miss Parkin, Miss Vowler and Miss Wood.

Cooking at a Training Camp at Pencalenick, Easter 1924.

1st Penzance Guides and Rangers at camp, Trewey St Levan in August 1930.

The camp at Trewey St Levan, took place around the time that the Guide uniform was changed. These changes incorporated changes in the hats and more fashionable shorter skirts. The hat badges that can be seen here were replaced by ones which showed the trefoil above the interlocked initials 'GG'.

1st Boscastle Guide Company on camp at Clovelly, August 1934. From left to right: Miss J. Lobb (Captain), Miss N. Mitchell (Lieutenant), Nina ?, Heather ?, Ellen ?, and Myrtle ?

Guides from North Cornwall at camp, Clovelly, August 1934. Nina Mitchell (in the second row, fourth from the left) made her Guide Promise during this camp.

Guides from the Truro area take part in a District Camp in 1946 or 1947. Back row, from left to right: Joan Harding. Front row, left to right: Janet Potter (3rd Truro St Georges), -?-, Shirley Gripe (1st Truro High School), -?-.

These Guides are obviously enjoying the comforts of their tent during their District Camp in 1946 or 1947.

These Cadets enjoy camp in their shelter at Boconnoc. From left to right:-?-, Glynis Johns and Bernice Gresswell around 1970s.

Unfortunately, the rain does not stop when the dinner needs to be cooked, as this photograph illustrates! The motto 'Be Prepared' is remembered here as a member of 10th Falmouth Guides cooks under the fire shelter at Condurro camp-site in September 1991.

10th Falmouth Guides stop for a rest at the Baden-Powell memorial stone on Brownsea Island, Dorset in 1995. The stone which commemorates the first experimental camp held on the site in August 1907 by Robert Baden-Powell, founder of the Scout and Guide Movements.

St Cleer Guides at Bocconoc during summer 2000. Back row, from left to right: Sam Lane and Natalie Hodge. Front row, from left to right: Rachel Humphries and Jenni Remnant.

The County Campsite, Condurro, is situated in the peaceful village of St Clement, Truro overlooking the Tresillian River. According to the campsite records, the first Guide camp took place in May 1939 and the site was donated to the Cornwall Guide Association by Francis T. Williams in May 1947.

Condurro has been a popular destination for many campers, including these Guides taking part in a training weekend in the late 1930s. Included on the far left is Grace Hocking.

CORNWALL GIRL GUIDES

County Camp Site—Condurro

ADDRESS.—Condurro, St. Clements, Truro.

SITE.—An old orchard, 1½ acres, 2 miles from Truro, overlooking Tresillian River.

WATER.—From Main Supply with tap in field.

WOOD.—To be picked up. Campers are asked to leave a reasonable wood pile for those who come after them.

SHELTER.—A wooden hut with platform 15 ft. x 20 ft. has been built, with an adjoining room for storage of equipment. Canvass screening can be hooked up in wet weather.

EQUIPMENT.—Tents, ground sheets and general equipment sufficient for 25 Guides and 4 Guiders are available.

QUALIFICATIONS.—

  Camping.—The usual qualifications are necessary.

  Bathing.—As the river is tidal, bathing is not very good, the river bed being very muddy. Usual qualifications (Grade " B ") as set out in P.O.R. and the Bathing and Boating leaflet, published at G.G.H.Q. are necessary.

  Boating.—Regulations required by G.G.H.Q. must be strictly observed. (See P.O.R. and Boating and Bathing Leaflet).

CHARGES (inclusive).—

  Guides.—6d. per head per night, 3/- per week.

  Rangers.—9d. per head per night, 4/6 per week.

  Guiders.—1/- per head per night, 6/- per week.

BOOKING FEE.—2/6 for week-ends, 5/- for week. This fee is returnable if withdrawal is made a fortnight before the date of the camp.

APPLICATIONS should be made to the Camp Site Recorder, **Mrs. Lanxon, Halcyon, Crescent Road, Truro.**

This poster for the County Camp Site at Condurro gives details to prospective campers of the location and facilities on offer. The site is maintained by a team of volunteers each year and now offers visiting campers an additional wooden building, shower and toilet block and electric lighting.

'Condo' the resident donkey at the Condurro campsite enjoys posing for this photograph. Sally Butler, County Camp Advisor, is to the left of centre in 1945. Also included: Elizabeth Lanxon and Norma 'Mini' Miners.

Guides and Guiders from Truro prepare for a visit from the Chief Guide, Lady Baden-Powell, at Condurro. Including Mrs Soloman (not in uniform), Joan Shingler, and Nina Bunney.

Members of the Wadebridge Trefoil Guild pictured outside the main hut at Condurro.

10th Falmouth Guides take up a popular position to pose on the steps of the main hut at Condurro in 1994.

The Service Camp has been held annually since 1976 and provides an opportunity for children who are considered in need of a holiday to enjoy the fun of camping with members of the Guide and Scout Associations in Cornwall. The children are enjoying a camp-fire.

For many of the children this is their first experience of camping, and may even be their first trip away from home. The aim of the Service Camp is to see them gain in confidence over the week and to send the children home with happy memories.

14th Truro Brownies tidying their beds on Pack Holiday at Cornwood in 1953.

At the same Pack Holiday at Cornwood, the Brownies enjoy playing a game outside.

These two photographs show how little Pack Holidays have changed over the years. Here three Brownies from 14th Truro enjoy fishing on Porth Beach, Newquay whilst on Pack Holiday in 1958.

Similarly, in this photograph (from left to right) Claire Carson, Nicola Pugh, Emma Sutton and Fiona Pugh from Threemilestone Brownies are enjoying playing on Crantock Beach during a Pack Holiday in 1990.

The Mount Edgcumbe Park during the 1986 Jamboree which was attended by 5,000

Guides and Scouts.

Hon. Betty Clay, daughter of Lord and Lady Baden-Powell, met the 10th Falmouth Guides during her visit to the Mount Edgcumbe Jamboree in 1986.

10th Falmouth Guides, part of the Tamar sub-camp, underneath their gateway at the Mount Edgcumbe Jamboree in 1986.

The Kernow '90 Jamboree and surrounding area which can be clearly seen in this aerial view of the Royal Cornwall Showground in August 1990.

The team of members of the Guide and Scout Associations who formed the Service Crew responsible for the marketing tent during Kernow '93. Included: George Heyworth and Maureen Vickers (Marketing Tent Chiefs).

10th and 11th Falmouth Guides beneath their flag at Kernow '93.

A group of Launceston Guides and Guiders, including Carly Durham (in wheelchair), join Helen Snelling (South West England Chief Commissioner) on a wet day at Kernow '93.

The Chief Guide, Bridget Towle, meets Guides at Kernow '97.

Jane Garside at Kernow '93 with, from left to right: Wendy Griffiths, Chris Grint and Jane Bennett.

St Cleer Guides with Leanne Stephenson (Young Leader) at Kernow '97.

Guides and Scouts join together with their standards for the Closing Ceremony at Kernow '97.

In 1957, one hundred years after the birth of Robert Baden-Powell, four World Camps were held. One of which was held in Windsor Great Park and was attended by 4,000 Guides from seventy different countries. A Cadet, a Ranger and five of the seven Guides chosen to represent Cornwall at this World Camp are seen here leaving Truro Railway Station at 5.30 a.m. From left to right: Priscilla Phillips, Kay Storey, Judith Harries, -?-, Janet Dwight, Jill Rookley and Angela Thomas. (Photograph appears courtesy of the *Western Morning News*)

One of the camp groups at the World Camp, staffed by representatives from Cornwall, included Ena Coombe, Betty Page, Ann Dunstan, Rosemary Anstis and Angela Thomas (Cadet).

Zita Morris, Deborah Downing and Emma Black on an International trip to Sangam in India, one of the World Centres, in July 1986.

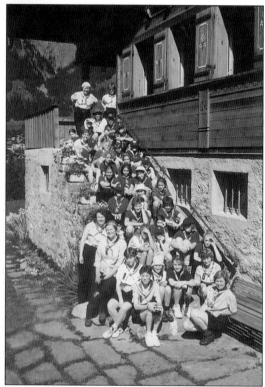

Guides and Guiders from Carrick South Division on the steps of another of the World Centres, Our Chalet in Switzerland, during an international trip in August 1992.

Five
Visitors to the County

The county of Cornwall has enjoyed visits by LadyBaden-Powell and many members of the Royal Family. This chapter will no doubt evoke many memories for the Brownies and Guides who have been privileged to have met these special visitors and will enable those readers who were not present to discover these occasions in the county's history.

Lady Baden-Powell at a Rally in Cornwall around the 1950s.

The Chief Guide visits the Guides at Truro High School, *c.* 1951.

These County Cadets and Sea Rangers waited on the platform of Bodmin Railway Station at dawn to meet Lady Baden-Powell during her visit to Cornwall in 1961.

Lady Baden-Powell visits Liskeard, April 1961. (Photograph appears courtesy of Mr J. Rapson)

Lady Baden-Powell meets Guides in St Ives, 1961.

Penzance Guides with Lady Baden-Powell in 1961.

During a visit to St Clement, Truro around 1961, Lady Baden-Powell met members of SRS *Venus* (Truro). Also included: Mrs Honor Blair, Mrs Phillips (District Commissioner, Truro), Lady Molesworth St Aubyn, Mrs Myra Bellingham and Miss Ena Coombe.

Lady Baden-Powell with Padstow Brownies at Wadebridge in 1961. Also included: Lady Molesworth St Aubyn, Daphne Hicks, Gillian Hewitt, Stephanie Thomas, Celia Vivian, Penny Sluman, Virginia Hellyar, Marta Thomas, Lorna Clapworthy (Brown Owl, Padstow), Councillor Thurston, Angela Murt, Elixabeth Hewitt, Elizabeth Clapworthy (Company Leader), Jane Taylor and Lara Reveley.

Daphne Hicks, carrying the 1st Padstow Brownie Pennant, meets Lady Baden-Powell during her visit to Bodmin in 1961. Also pictured are Elizabeth Clapworthy (Company Leader), Lorna Clapworthy (Brownie Guider), and Brownies Gillian Hewitt, Celia Vivian, Penny Sluman and Marta Thomas. (Photographs appear courtesy of the *Western Morning News*)

These Brownies from Wadebridge are enjoying the opportunity to talk to Lady Baden-Powell in 1961.

Margaret Harris and Rosemary Edmonds from Liskeard, greet Lady Baden-Powell in 1951.

Lady Baden-Powell with some of the Guides who surprised her as she landed at Penzance Heliport following a visit to the Isles of Scilly in the 1960s. From left to right: Wendy Tresidder, June Simpson, Ann Williams, Lady Baden-Powell, Margaret Hodge, Pat Williams and Judith Penrose.

Lady Baden-Powell with the Brownies and Guides from the Isles of Scilly during a visit in the 1960s. Also included: Mrs Ena Reseigh (District Commissioner, Isles of Scilly), Hon. Mrs Betty Clay and Mrs Elizabeth Legg (Brownie Guider).

Mrs B. Page and Mrs R. Cornish talk to Her Majesty The Queen during her visit to Liskeard in 1955. Also included, the Mayor of Liskeard, Mr Snell.

Her Majesty The Queen inspecting the line-up of members of the youth organisations during her visit to Truro in 1956. The buildings in the background include the Red Lion Hotel prior to the accident in 1967 when a runaway lorry crashed through the front of the building.

Her Majesty The Queen pictured with Mrs Phyllis Read (Assistant County Commissioner) during her visit to Truro in May 1956.

Brownies Valerie Dobson and Cathleen Martin offer flowers to Her Majesty Queen Elizabeth, The Queen Mother at the Royal Cornwall Show, held at Merrymeet near Liskeard in 1959. Also included: Sir John and Lady Molesworth St Aubyn.

Her Majesty, Queen Elizabeth meets some Guides from St Ives during a visit to Truro in 1962.

Her Royal Highness Princess Margaret meets Margaret Jackson (District Commissioner, Liskeard) and the Guides of Liskeard during her visit in July 1973.

1st Liskeard Brownies show Her Royal Highness Princess Margaret the flags tey had made during her visit in July 1973. (Photographs appear courtesy of Mr J. Rapson)

Her Majesty Queen Elizabeth The Queen Mother meets some Brownies on Falmouth Pier in July 1985. From left to right: Chris Grint, Anita Percival, Juliet ?, Jacqueline Allday, Sarah Richards, Catherine Mistlebrook, Heidi Birch, Lucy Badger, -?-, Sarah Van Den Helival.

Her Royal Highness Princess Margaret inspecting the Guard of Honour during her visit to the Royal Cornwall Show at Wadebridge Showground.

Her Royal Highness The Princess Royal meets 2nd Fowey Guides, watched by Mia Girling (Guider) and Rosemary Richards (Assistant Guider) around May 1990.

Her Royal Highness The Princess Royal accepts a bouquet of flowers from Isabel Mulley (a Bodmin Guide) and Angela Thomas (County Commissioner) during her visit to the Royal Cornwall Show around early 1990s. (Photograph appears courtesy of the *Western Morning News*)

Her Majesty The Queen meets Coralie Goodfellow during her visit to the Royal Cornwall Show in June 2000. Also included are Lady I. Molesworth (Show President) and Jonathan Coode (Chairman of the Royal Cornwall Agricultural Association).

His Royal Highness The Duke of Edinburgh meets the Guides of the Messenger Service at the Royal Cornwall Show in June 2000.

Six
2000 ...and Then?

The year 2000 was celebrated in many different ways across the world and members of the Guide Association held their own celebrations to mark the turning of the Millennium. In Cornwall a variety of events took place from small celebrations in each unit, to larger activities which joined members together from all over the county. These photographs show a selection of the county-wide activities and events which bring the history of Guiding in Cornwall up to date to the year 2000.

One of the events that took place to celebrate the year 2000, was a festival day for members of the Guide and Scout Associations in Cornwall held at Stithians Showground. Over 3,500 members joined together for the day in June. This aerial photograph shows the '2000' formation made by the Guide and Scout Sections.

A Thinking Day 2000 Dove was hung in Truro Cathedral, made by Jeff Askew and Peter Clark on behalf of the Cornwall Guides to symbolize peace and unity. Made from polystyrene, it had a wing span of 8ft and was covered with approximately 6,000 tissue-paper hands cut out by all of the members of the Cornwall Guide Association.

The dove is seen here being unloaded from the Royal Mail lorry at High Cross, Truro before being hung in the nave of the Cathedral by local firemen in preparation for the Thinking Day Service on 19 February 2000.

The cast of 'The Rainbow People' who performed at the Thinking Day Service in Truro Cathedral. The play was directed by Susan Odgers and Jean Whetham and narrated by Helen Downing and Sarah Littler. The cast was formed from members of 12th Truro Guides, 8th Truro Brownies, 1st Perranarworthal Brownies and 1st Four Lanes Brownies.

Guiding members from around the South West England Region joined together for 'Guiding on the Move' in August 2000. The single-decker bus, pictured here, travelled from Cornwall, through the counties of south-west England and finally arriving at the Region Headquarters in Salisbury.

Pictured with the bus at the entrance to Flambards Theme Park, near Helston, are Rosemary Dibden (South West England Chief Commissioner), Mayor of Helston and Tiffany Truscott (BBC *Radio Cornwall*).

After a journey of eighty-one miles, this is at Lanhydrock House with members of the North Cornwall Division.

As the bus travelled through Cornwall, the Guides and Leaders travelling in it joined in activities such as singing, making a friendship chain and colouring a map of the journey. Included in this photograph at Lanhydrock House are Margaret Flinders (Region PR Advisor), Rosemary Dibben (SW England Chief Commissioner), Jane Bennett (County Commissioner), Tricia Pilkington (Cornwall's Co-ordinator for the bus) and Sylvia Sanders (County PR Advisor).

1st St Budock and 2nd Falmouth Brownies join together in July 2000 with their Guiders Pauline Allday and Pam Sjoholm, in order to take part in their Walking through the Millennium and Friendship Web challenges.

1st St Austell and 6th St Austell Brownies enjoyed a day trip to Respryn and Lanhydrock House as part of the Friendship Web Challenge in October 2000.

A special event, Gig2K, was organized for members of the movement at the Millennium Dome, London in November 2000. Guides from 14th Truro and 1st Threemilestone joined the thousands of Brownies and Guides from across the UK for this event.

Truro Rangers renew their Promise at Gig2K in November 2000 held at the Millennium Dome. From left to right: Jody Woolcock, Lisa Goodman, Ann Kitaruth (Guider), Bridget Towle (Chief Guide), Dawn Indge, Jo Wright (District Commissioner, Gloweth), Katie Newton.

Each Guide county in the South West England Region was asked to embroider an image for a panel to celebrate the Millennium. Designed by Carol Phillips, the Cornish panel took nine months to complete and now hangs in the Region Headquarters at St Ann's Manor, Salisbury. The embroidery was completed by Josie Bee, Elizabeth Bee, Jane Bennett, Elizabeth Doney, Jan King, Kay Light, Micky Mitchell, Nina Mitchell, Julie Row, Valerie Ruse, Jean Tamblyn and Cynthia Tonkin.

(b)

(a)

(c)

For many of the events that took place to celebrate the year 2000 a badge or keepsake was designed for those who took part. Here are just a few of the badges: a) Awarded to members of Cornwall Guides who completed the challenges for the Friendship Web 2000; b) given to all those from the Guide and Scout Associations who attended the Millennium activity day and camp at Stithians Showground in August 2000 and c) GIG2K, given to all those who attended the event held at the Millennium Dome.

128